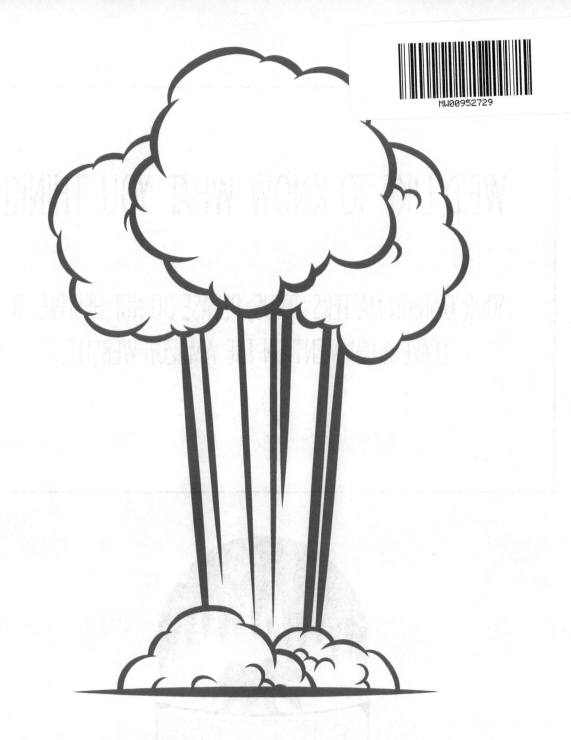

THIS COLORING BOOK BELONGS TO:

_____

_____

WE'D LIKE TO KNOW WHAT YOU THINK!

YOUR OPINION MATTERS TO US, PLEASE DO NOT HESITATE TO LEAVE A COMMENT ON THE AMAZON WEBSITE.

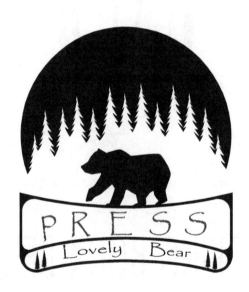

COLOR TEST PAGES

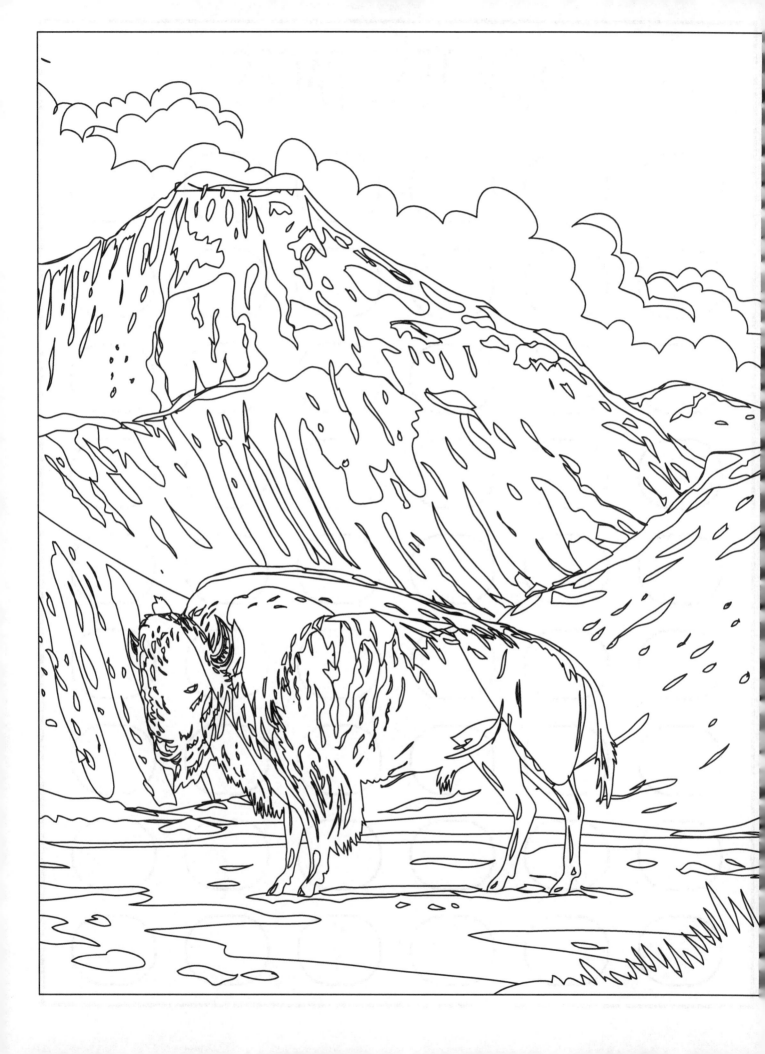

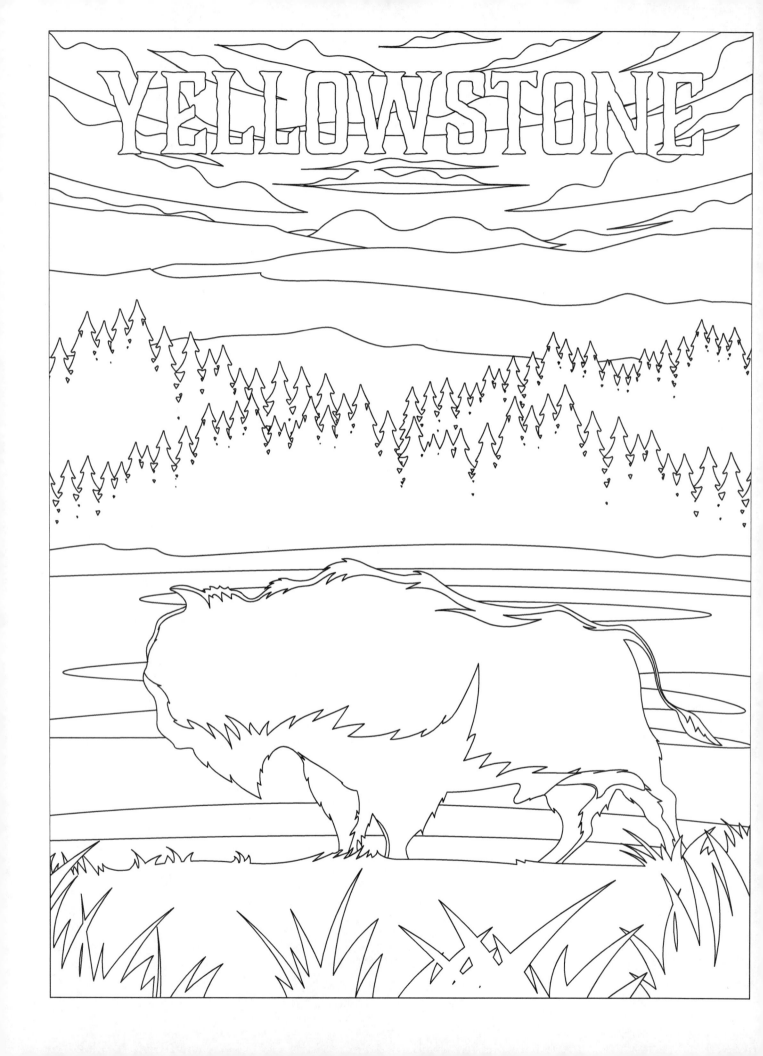

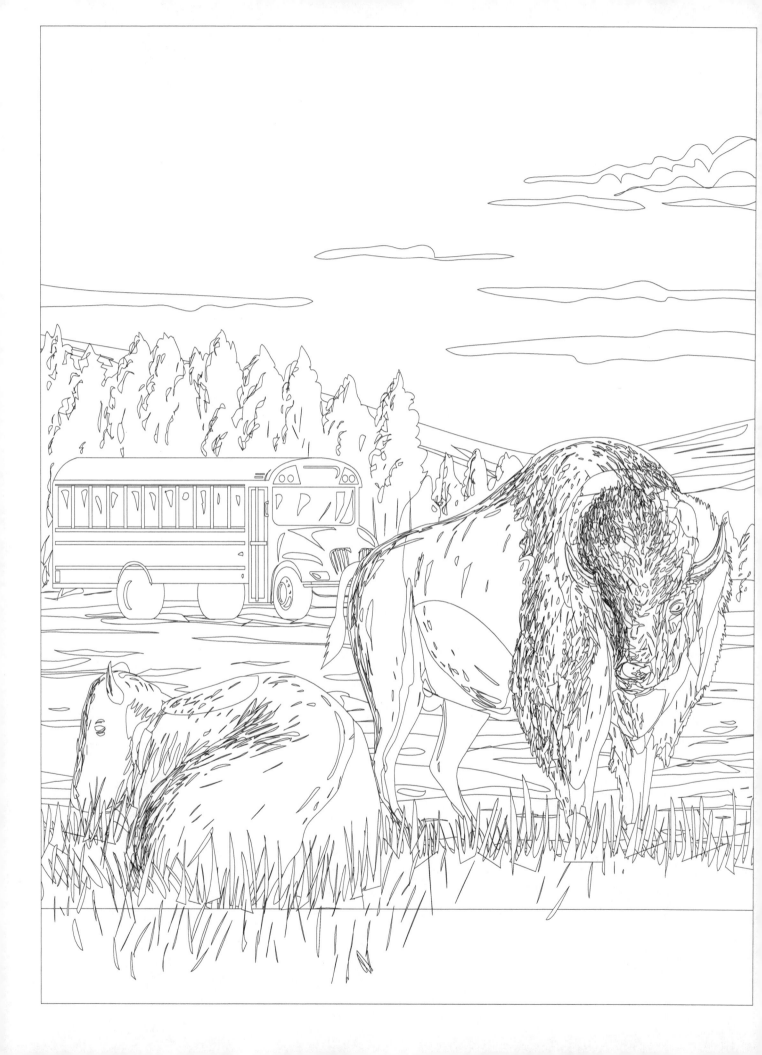

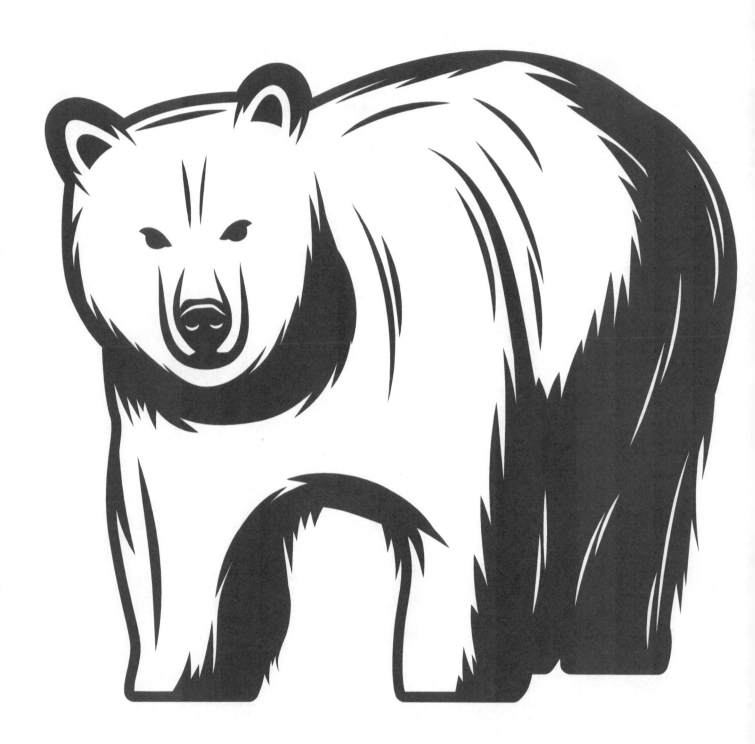

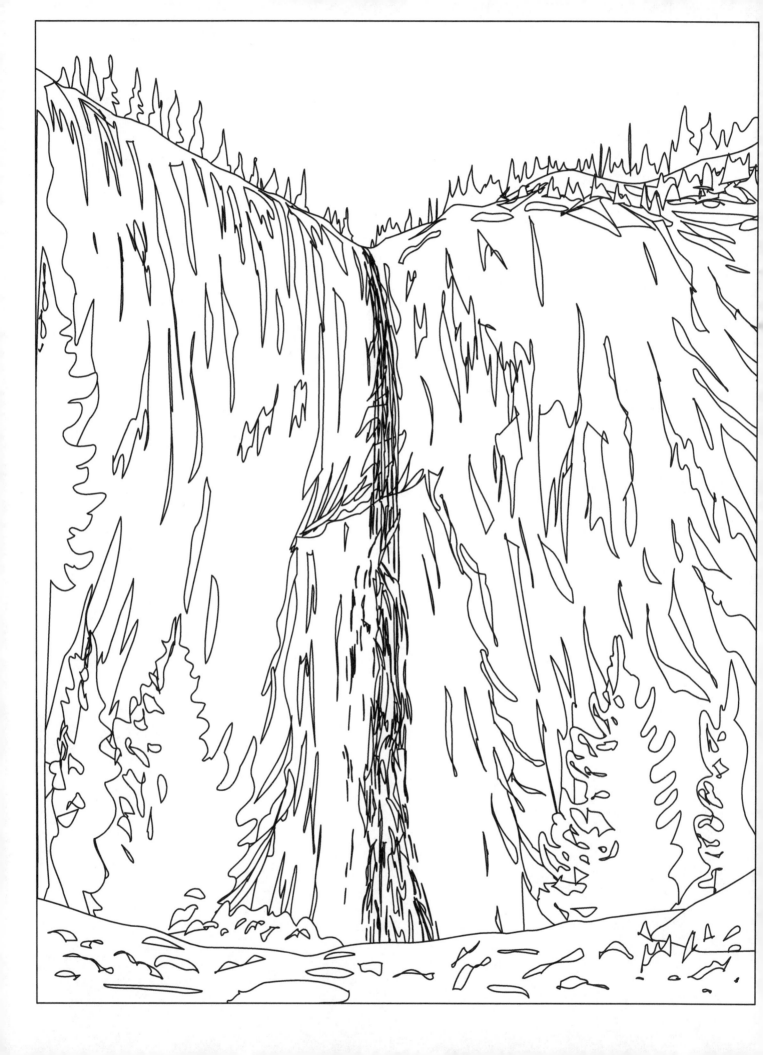

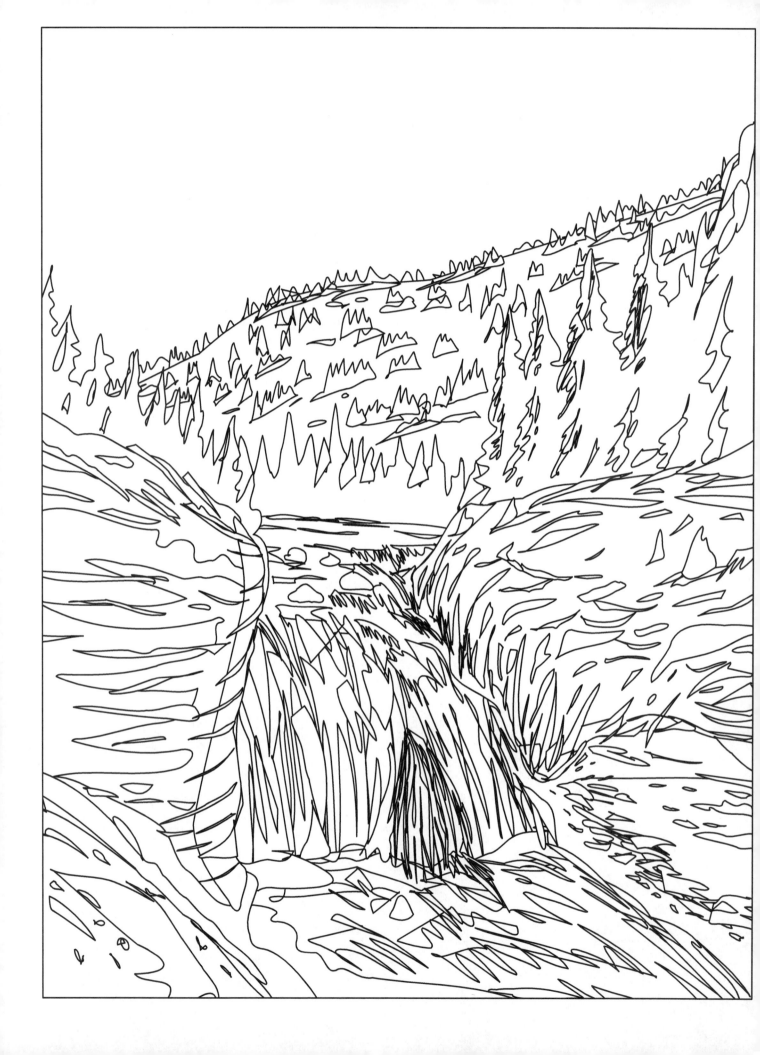

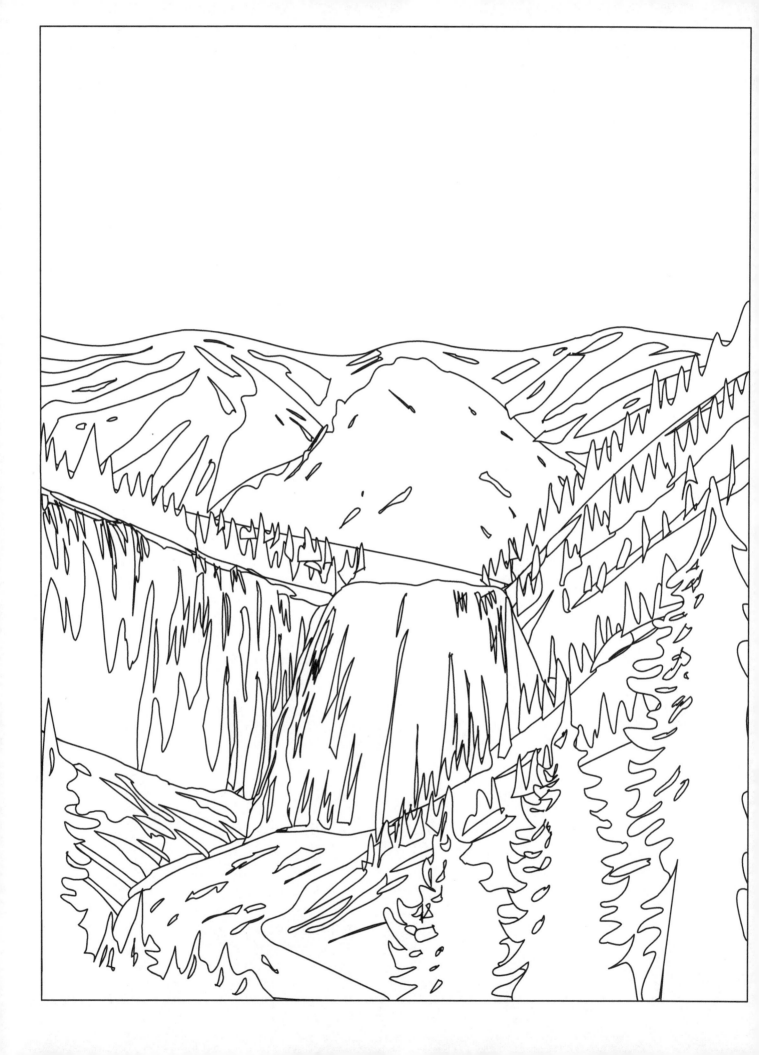

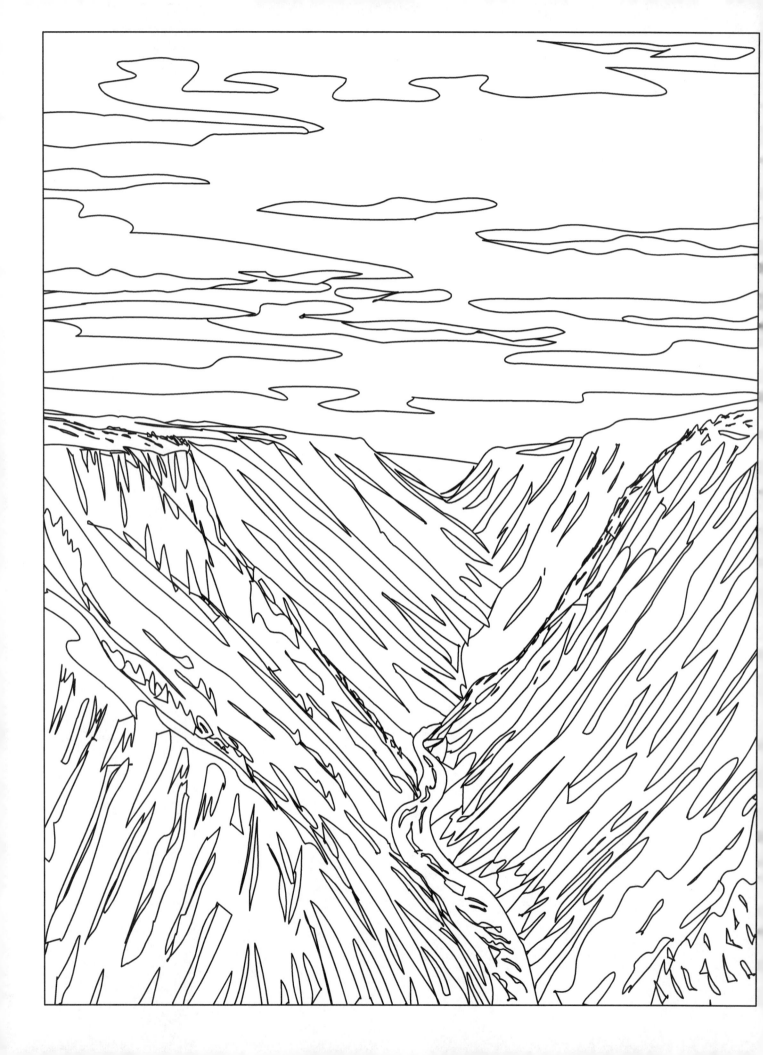

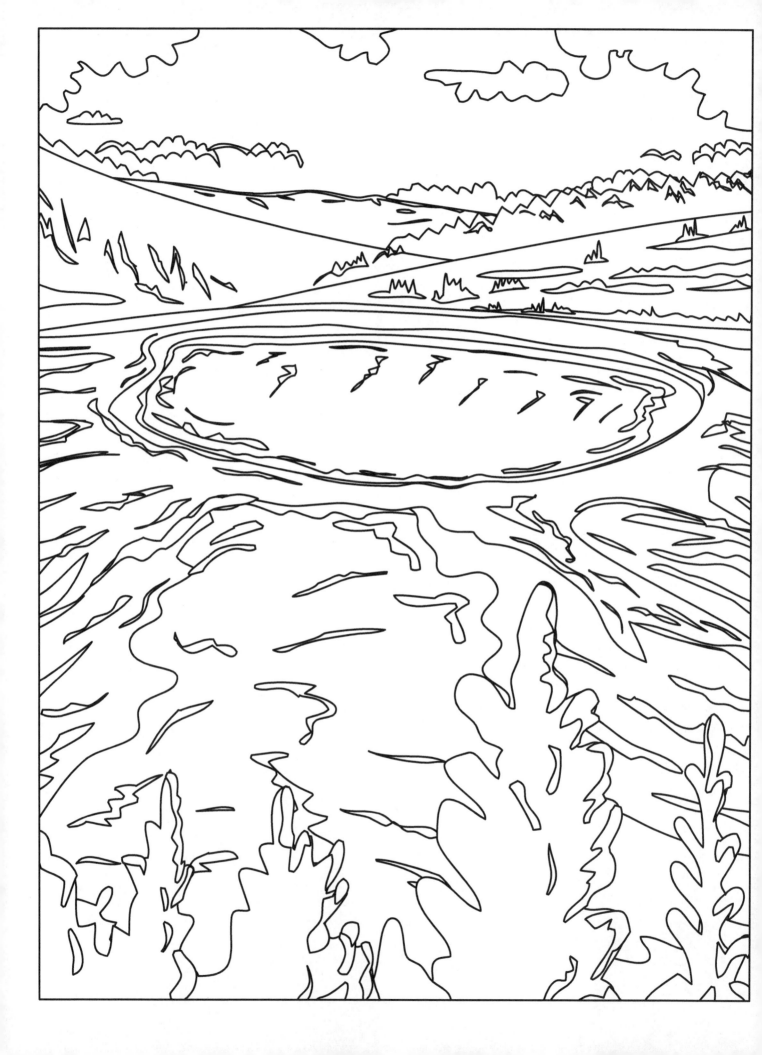

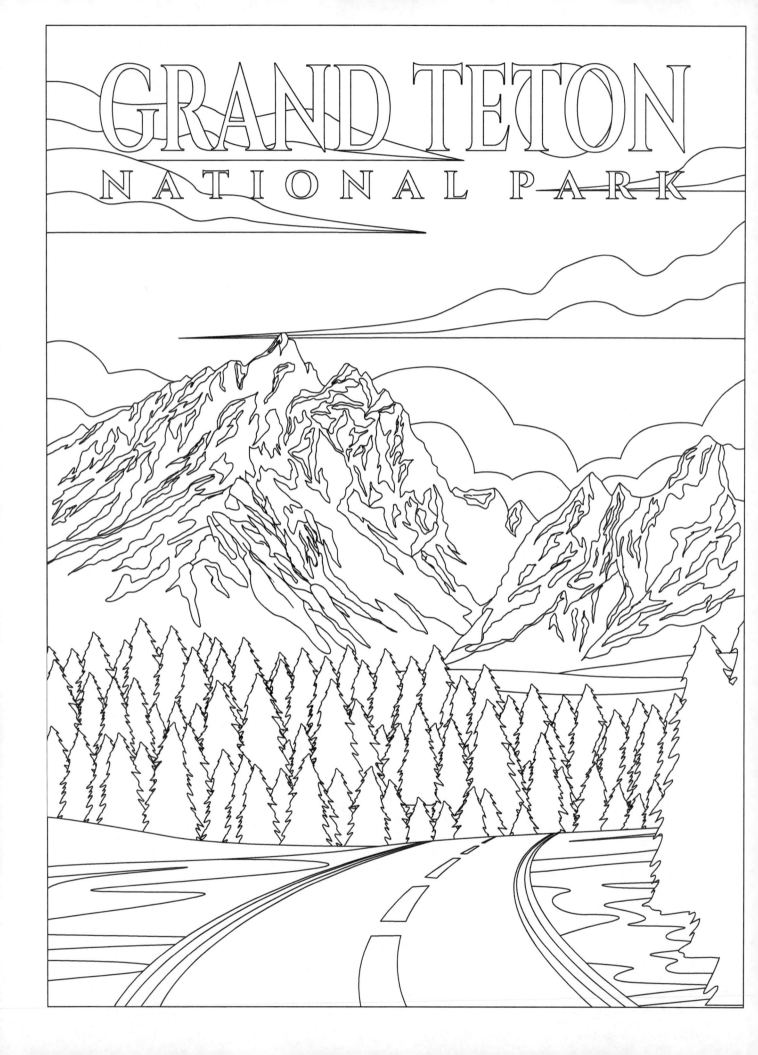

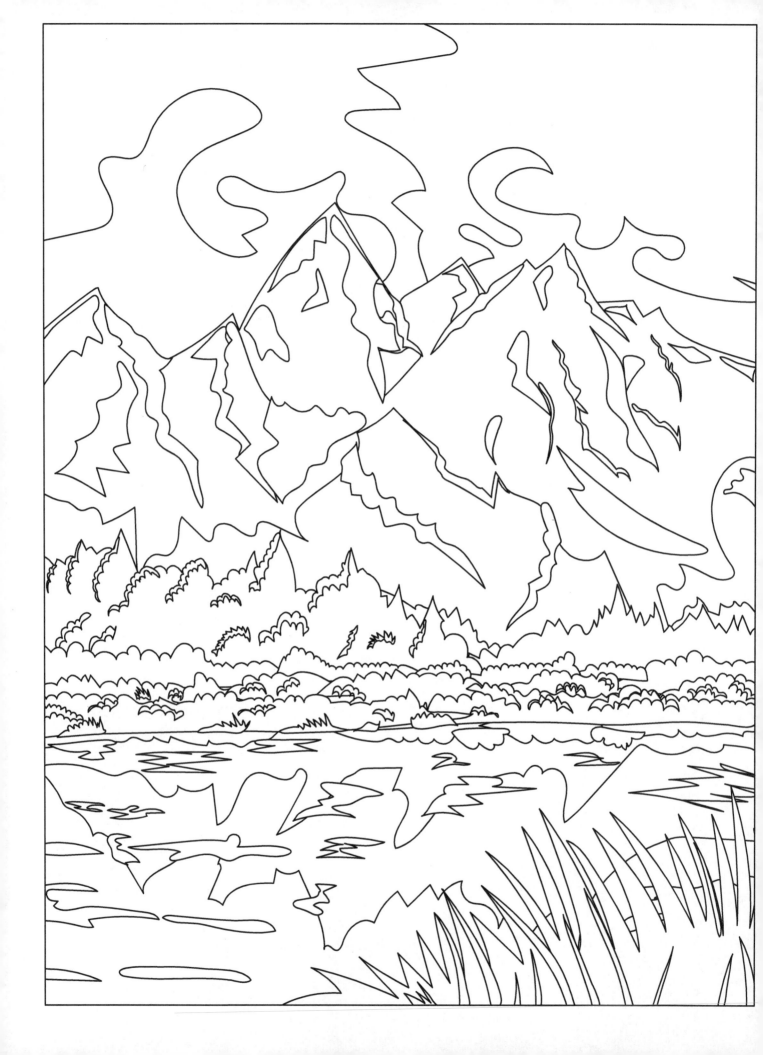

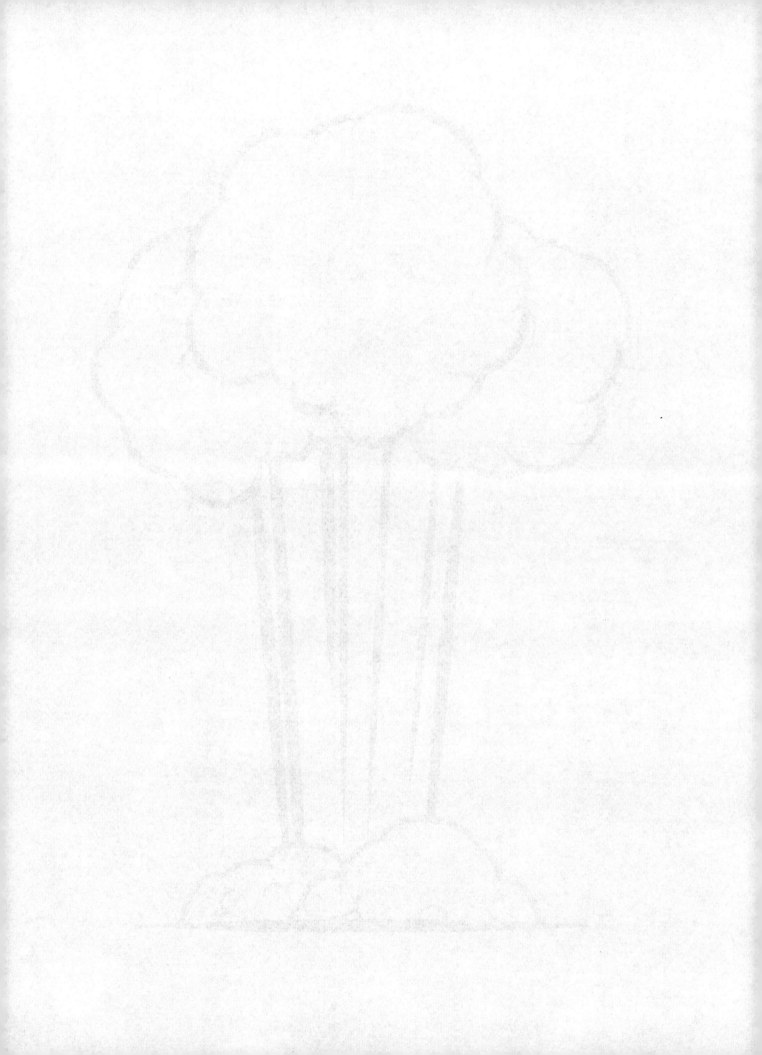

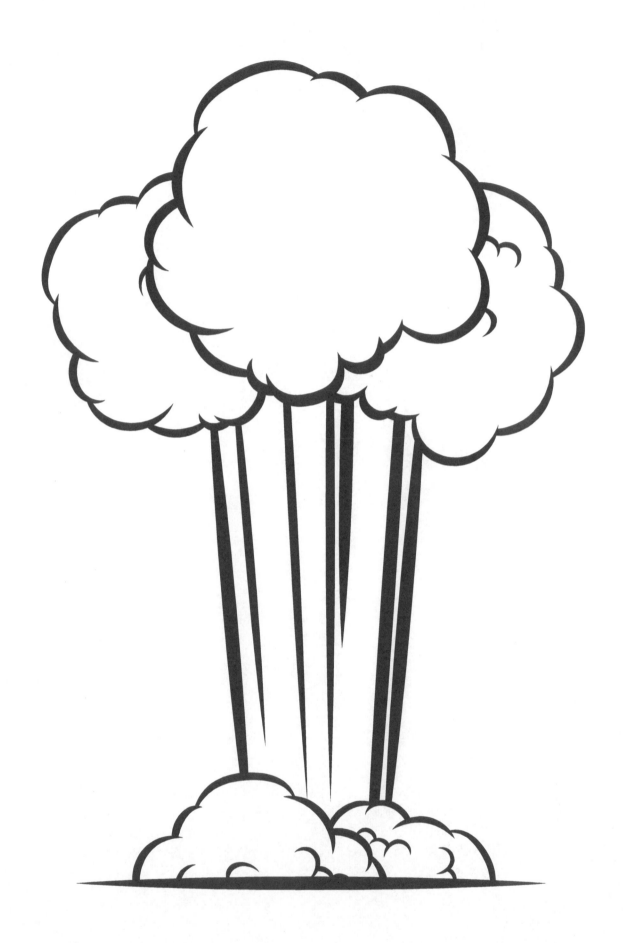

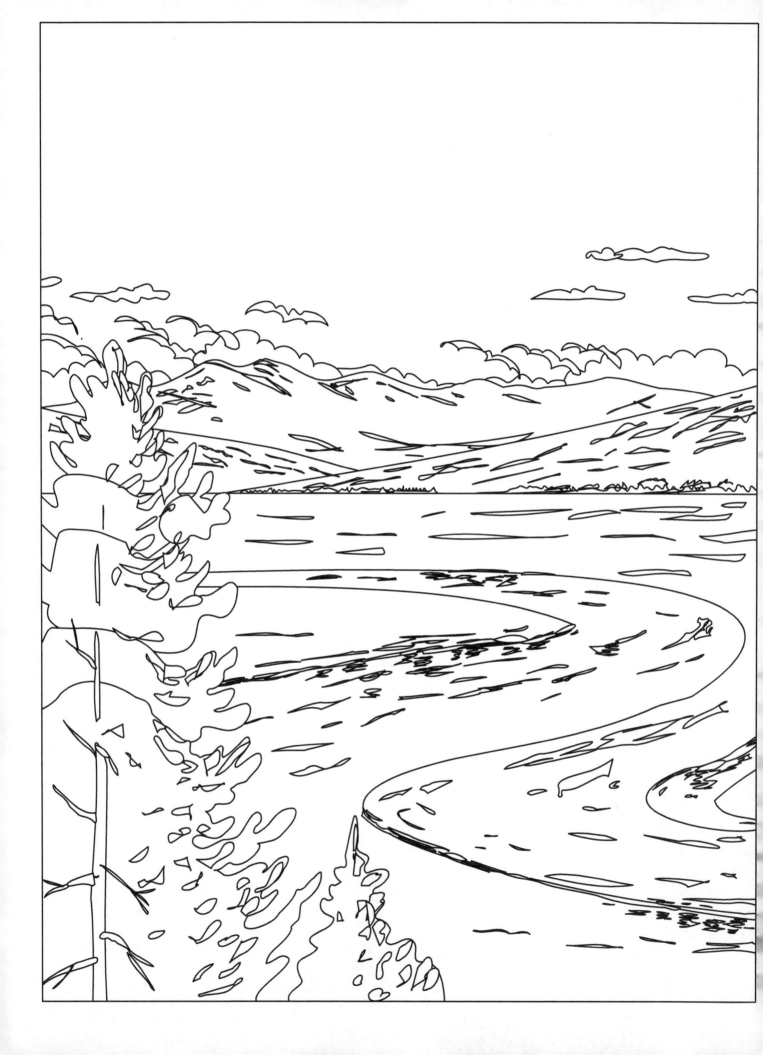

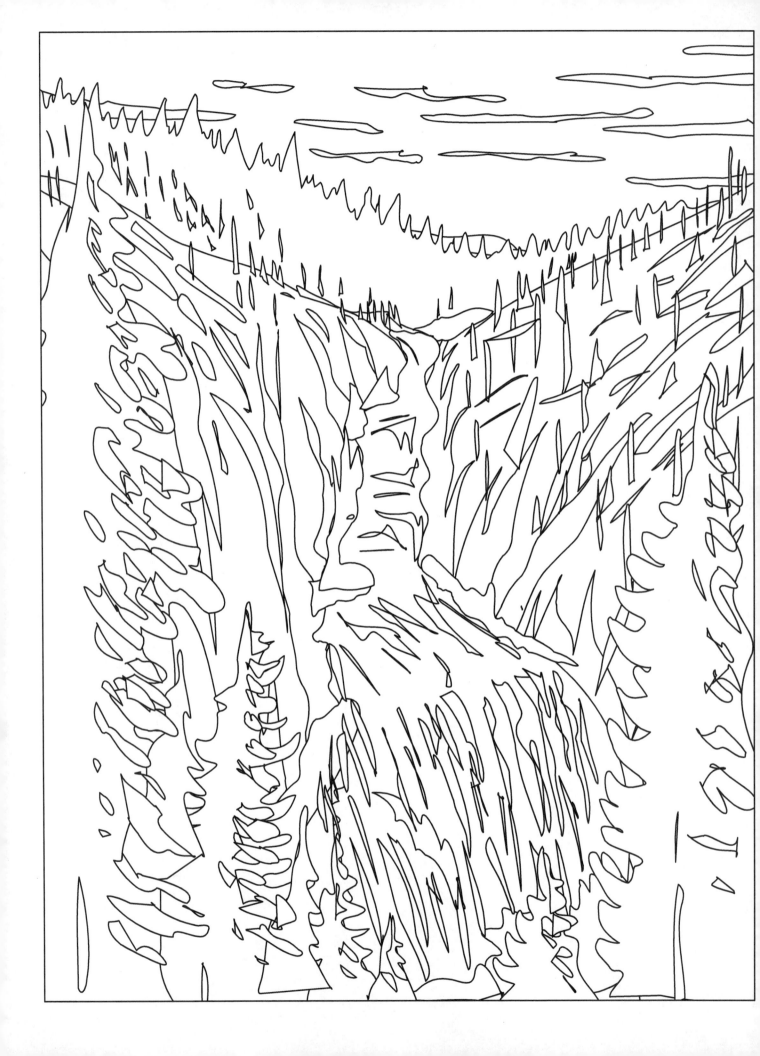

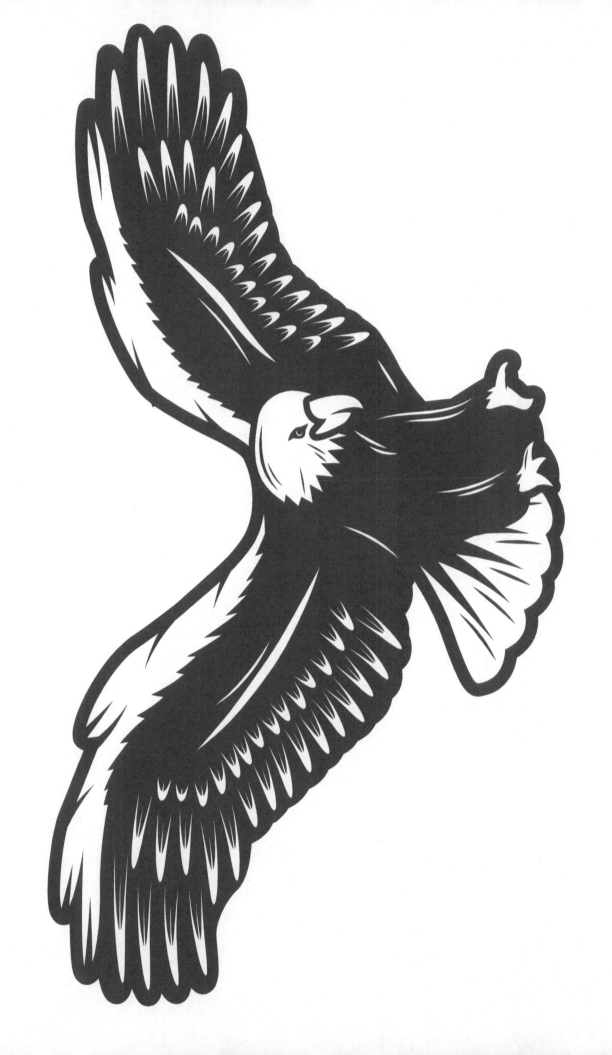

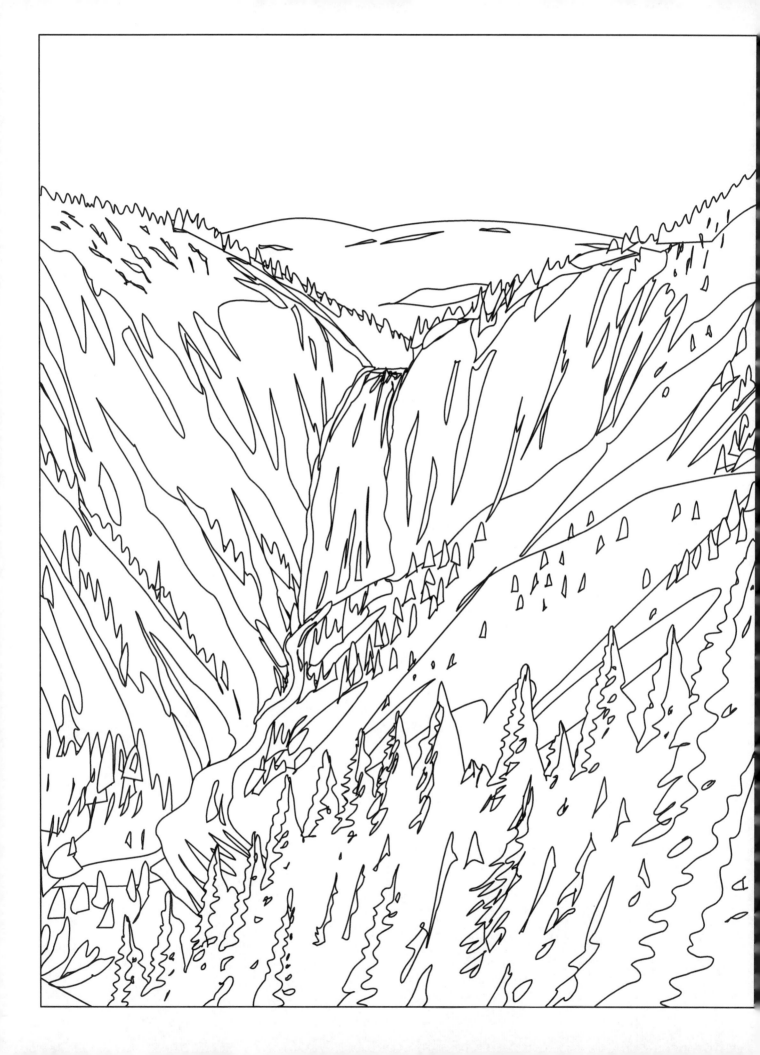

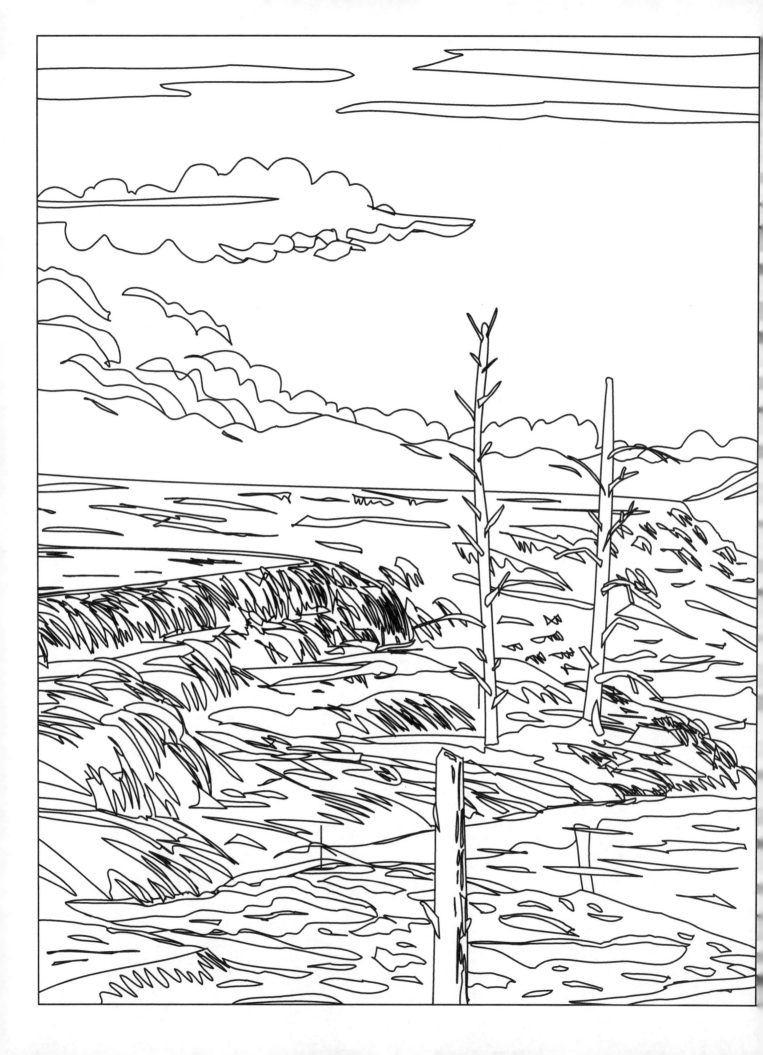

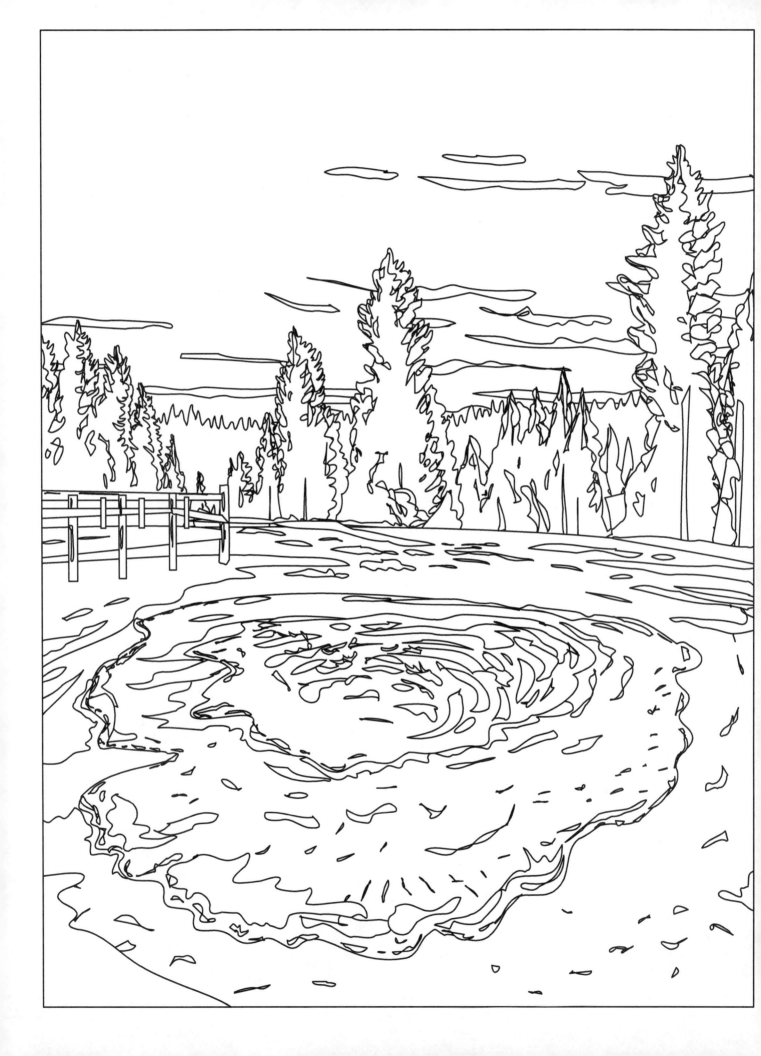

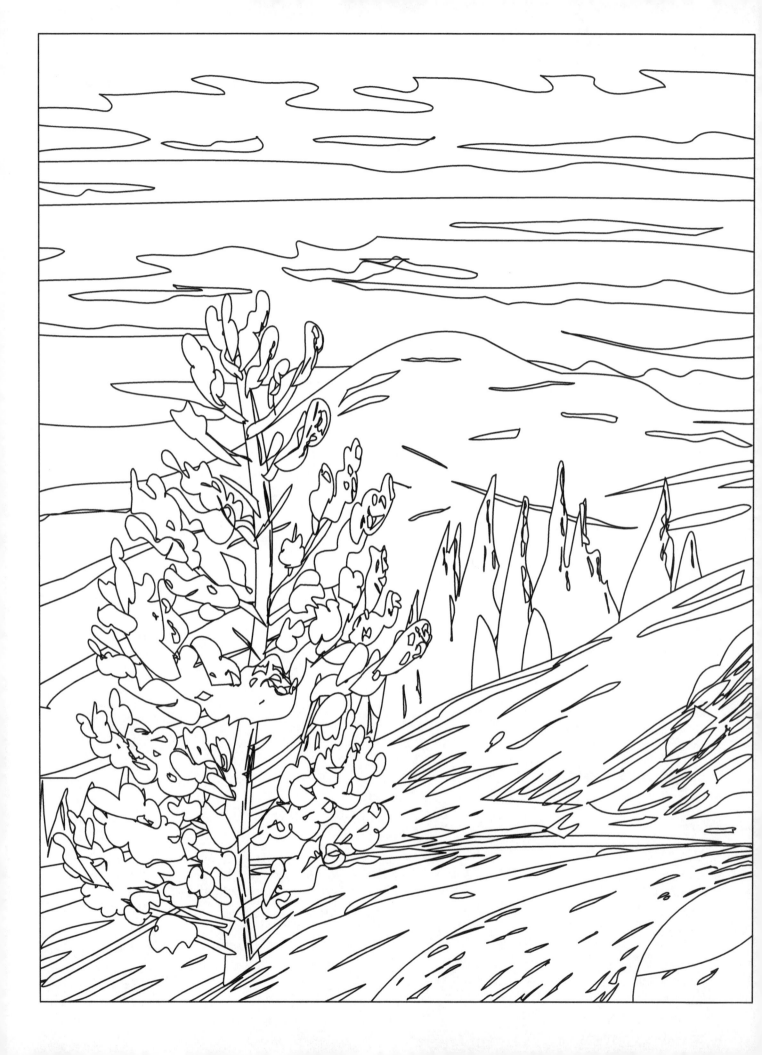

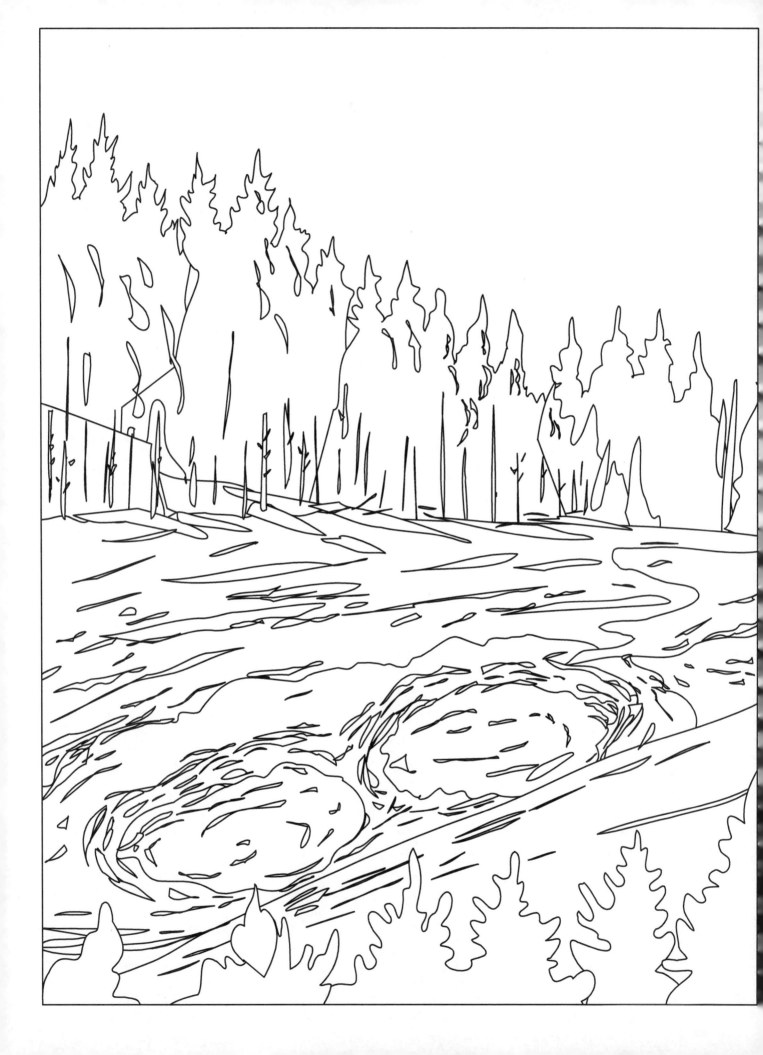

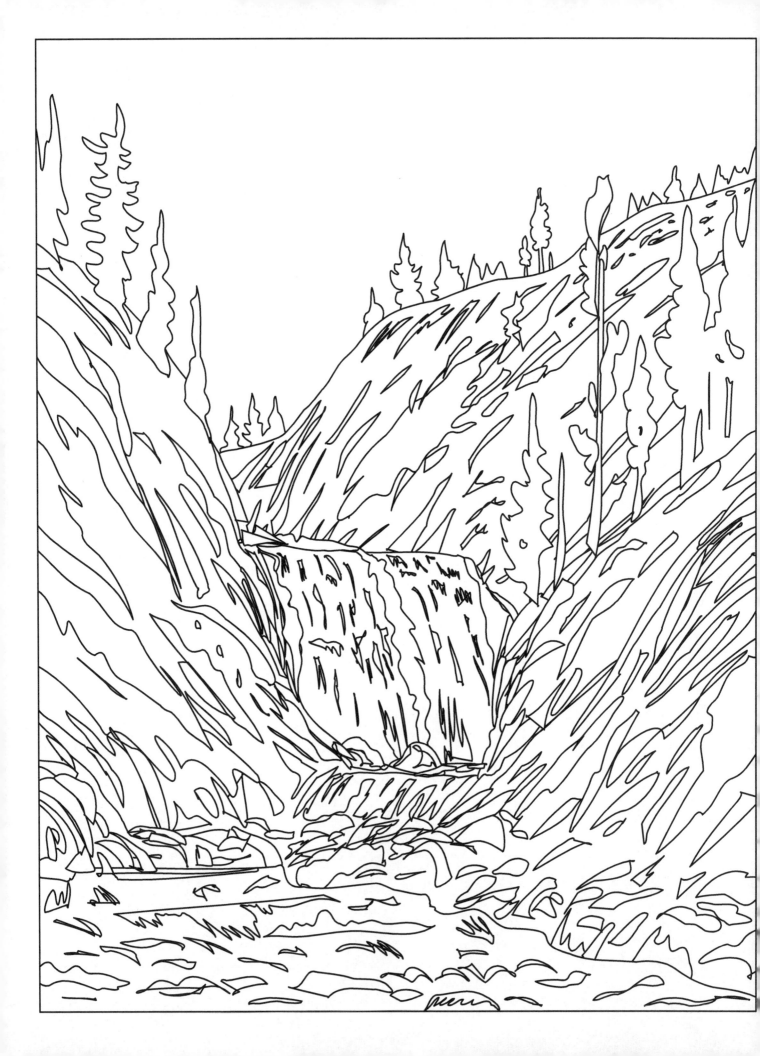

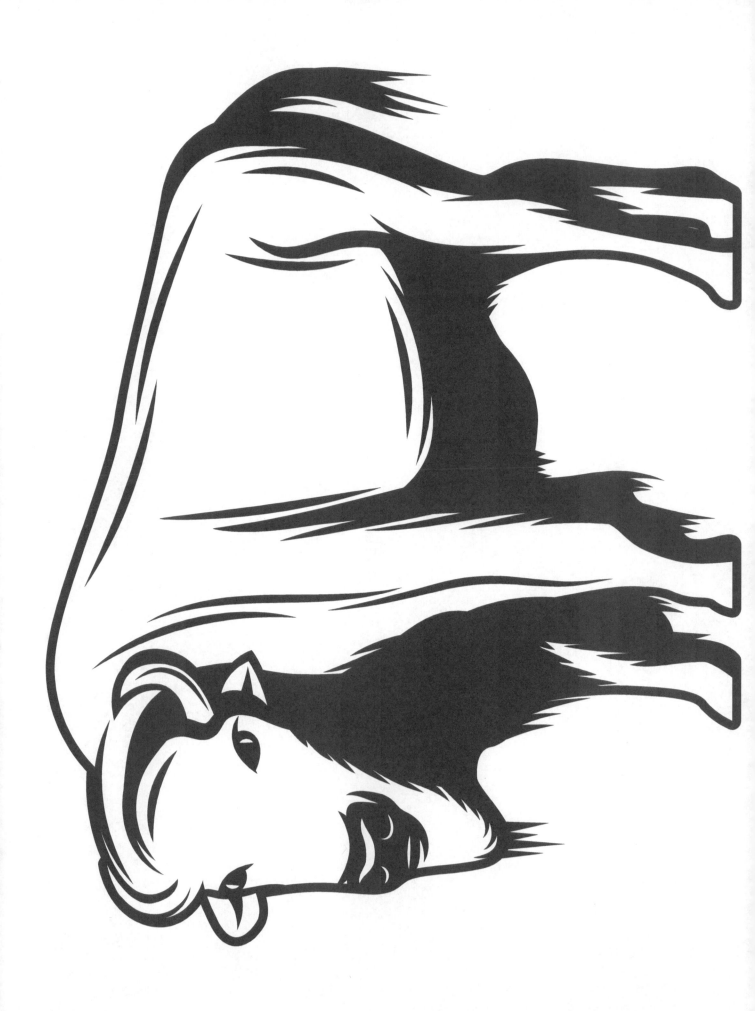

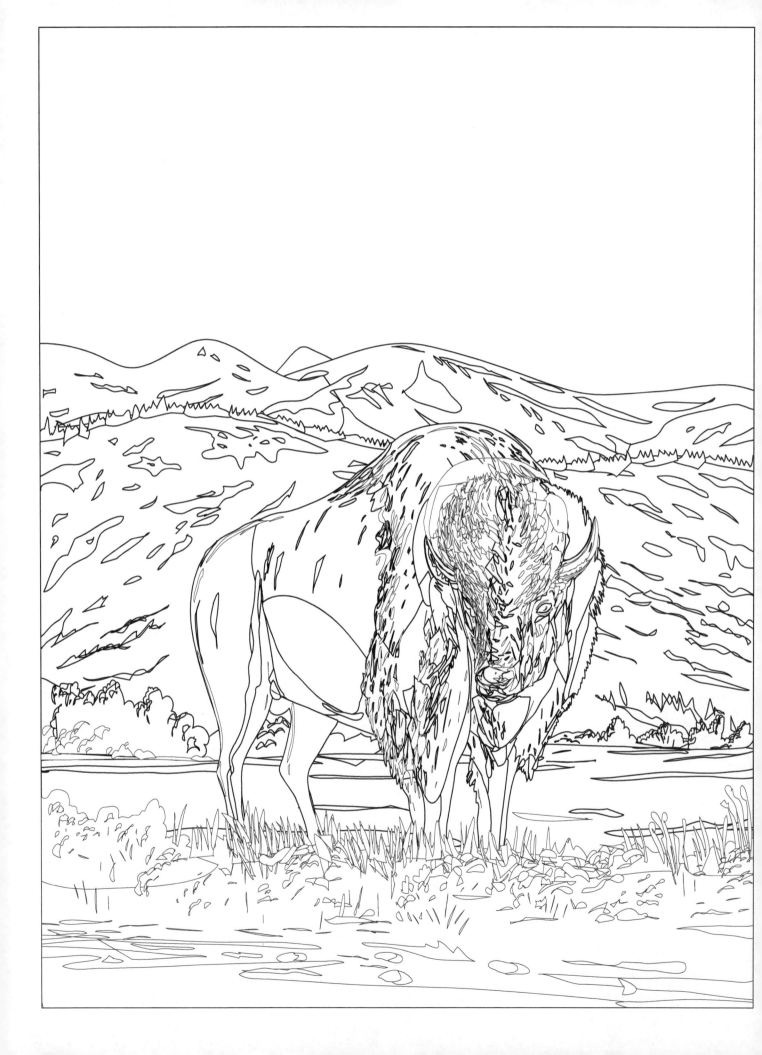

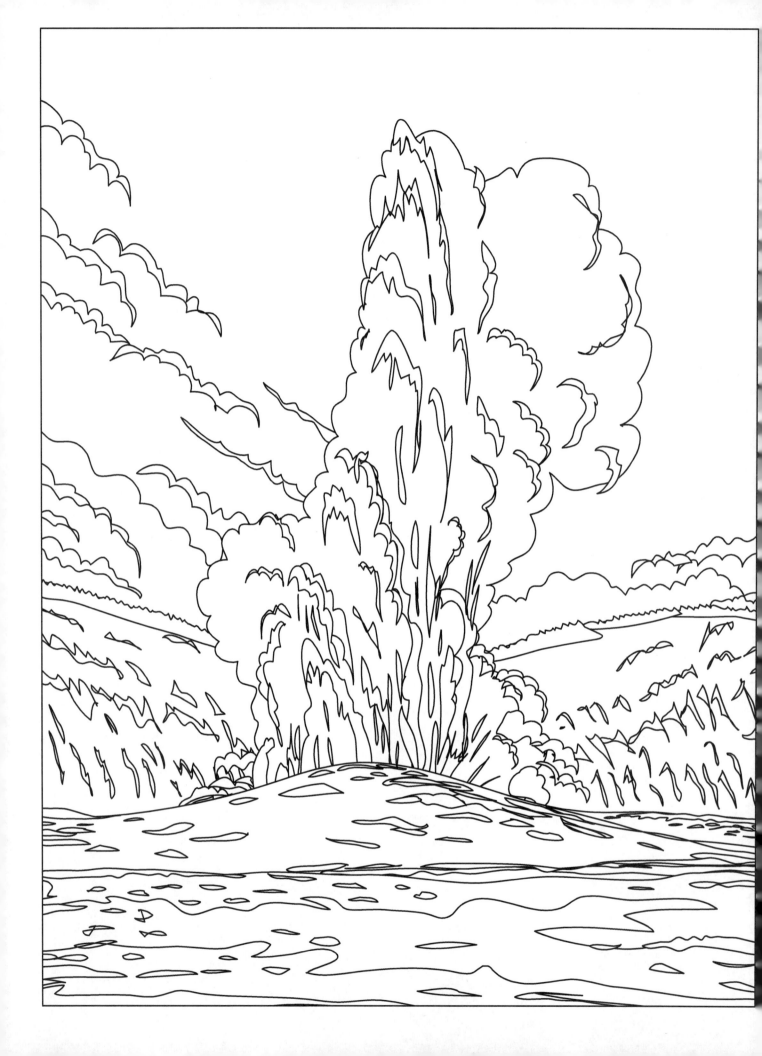

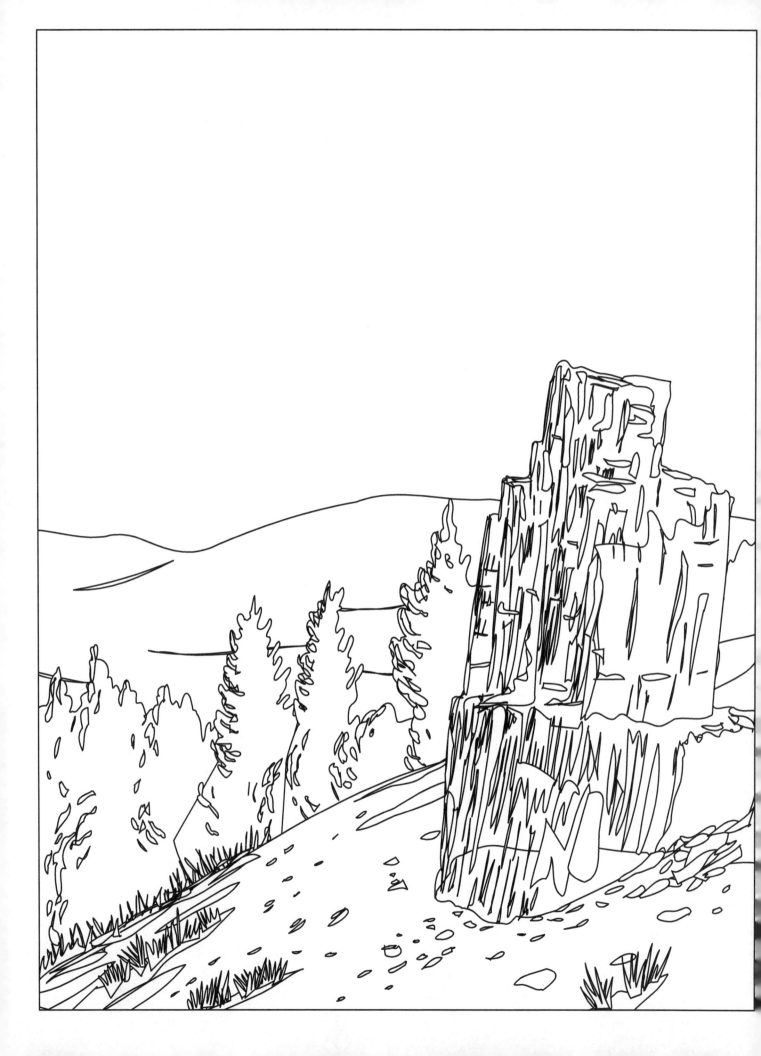

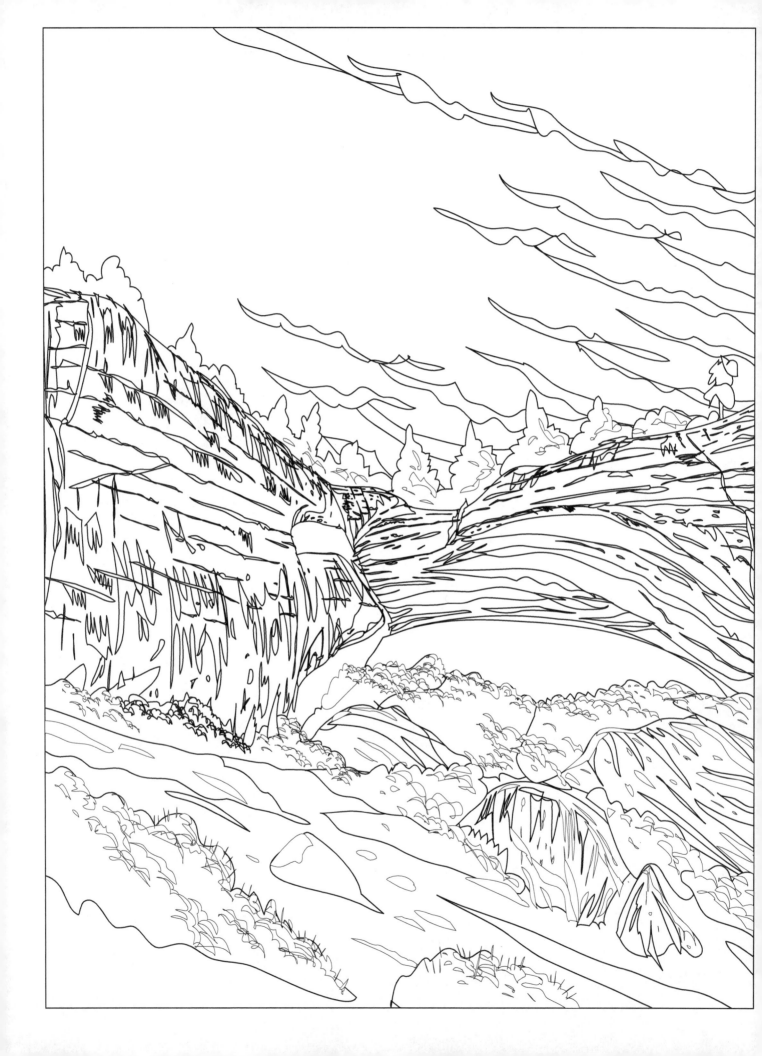

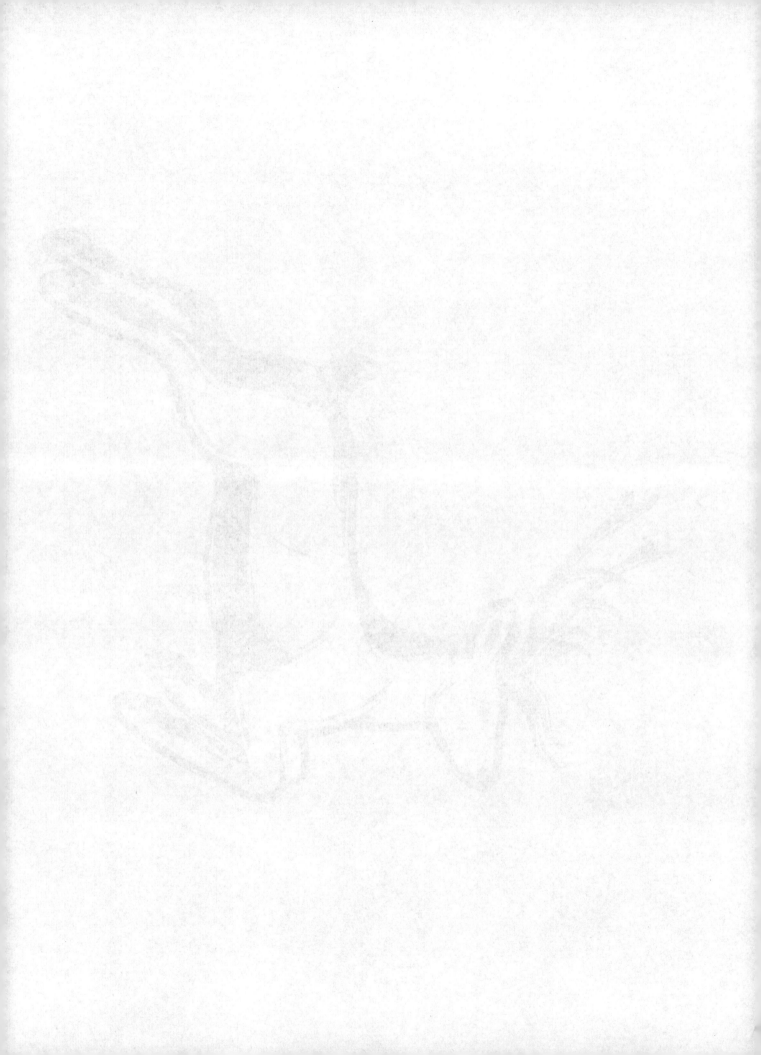

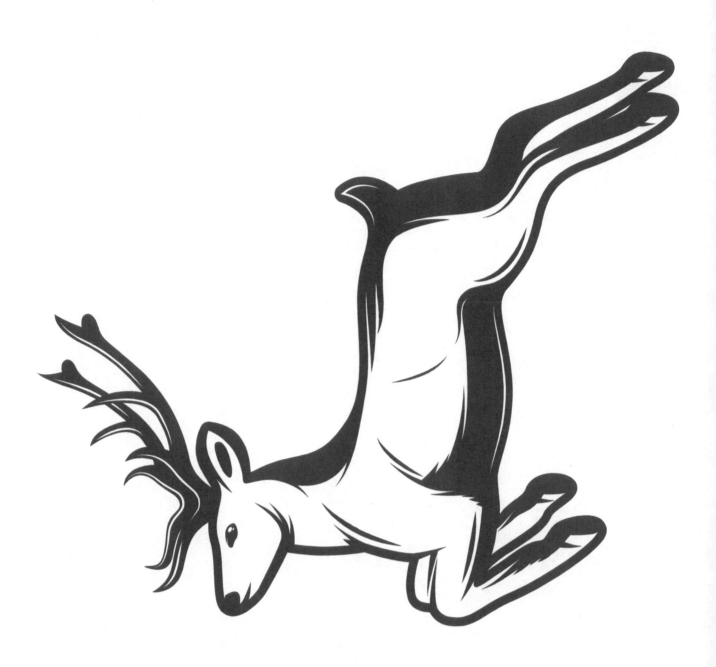

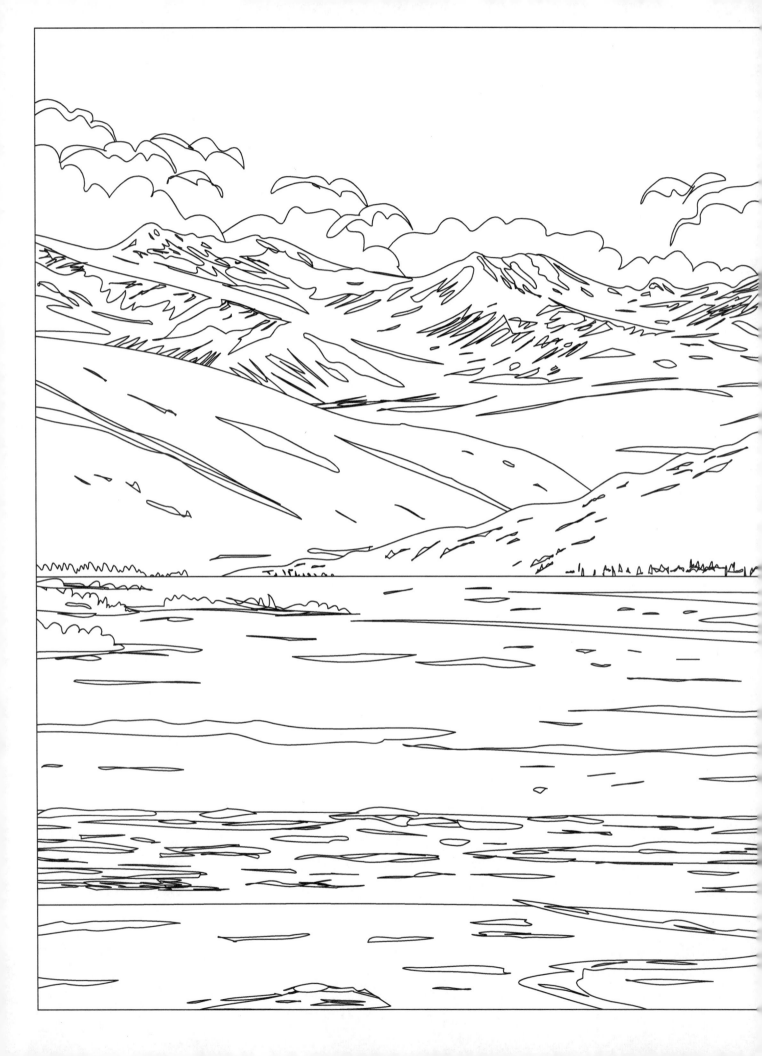

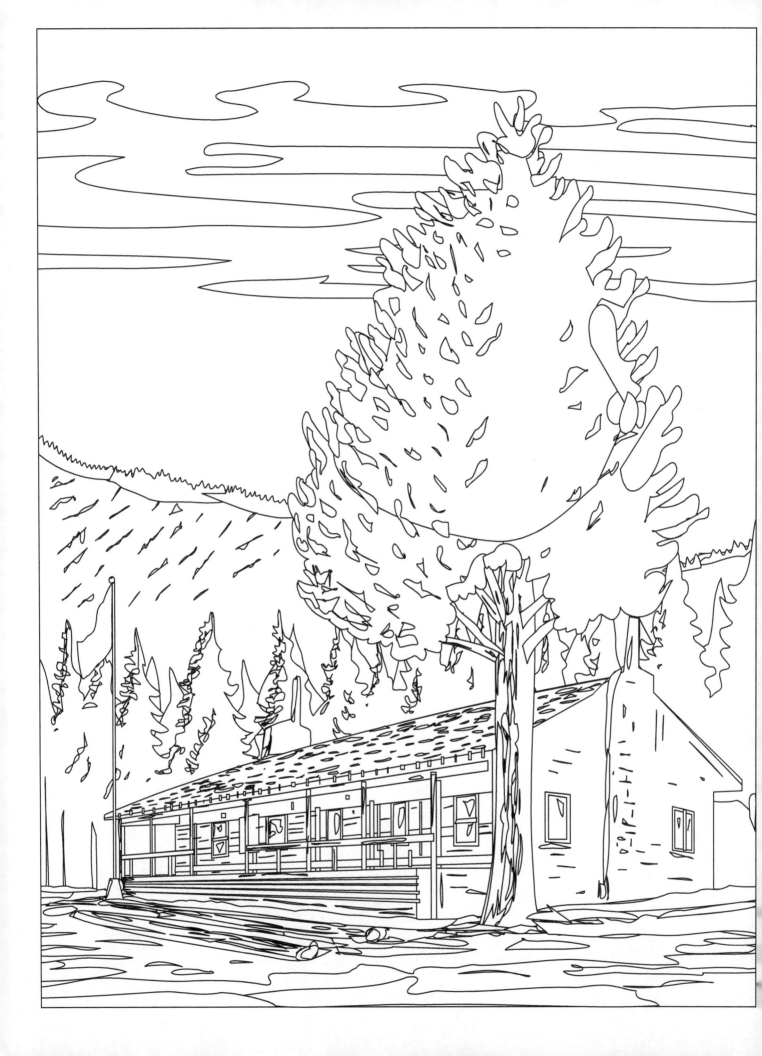

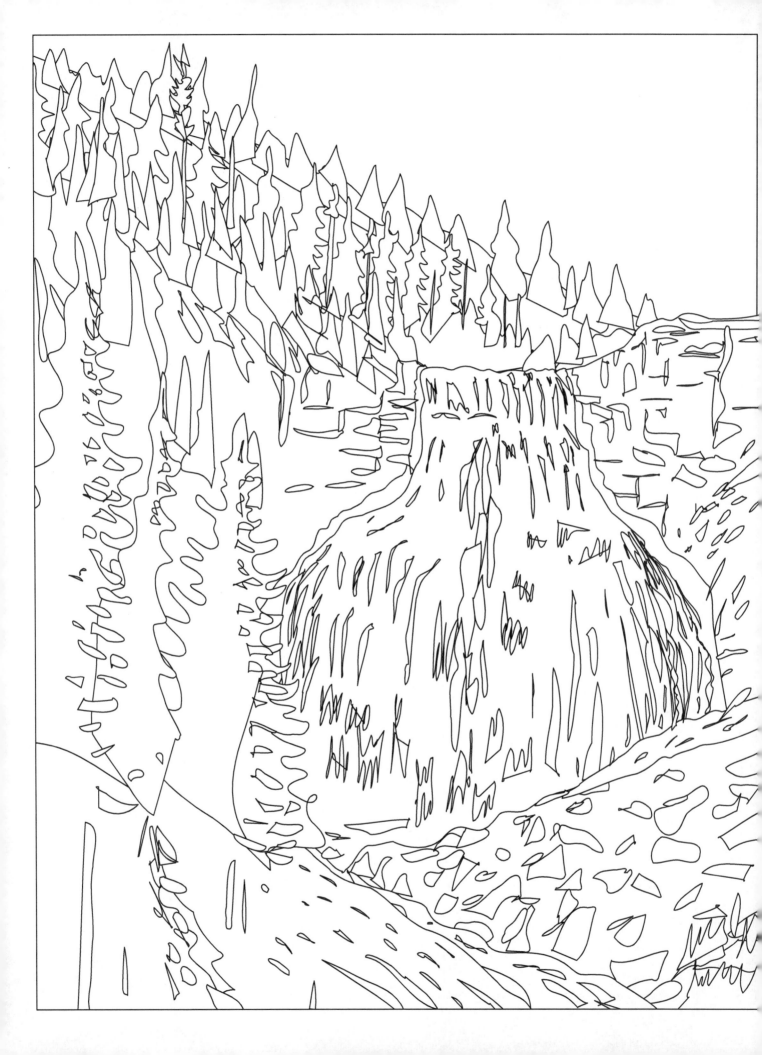

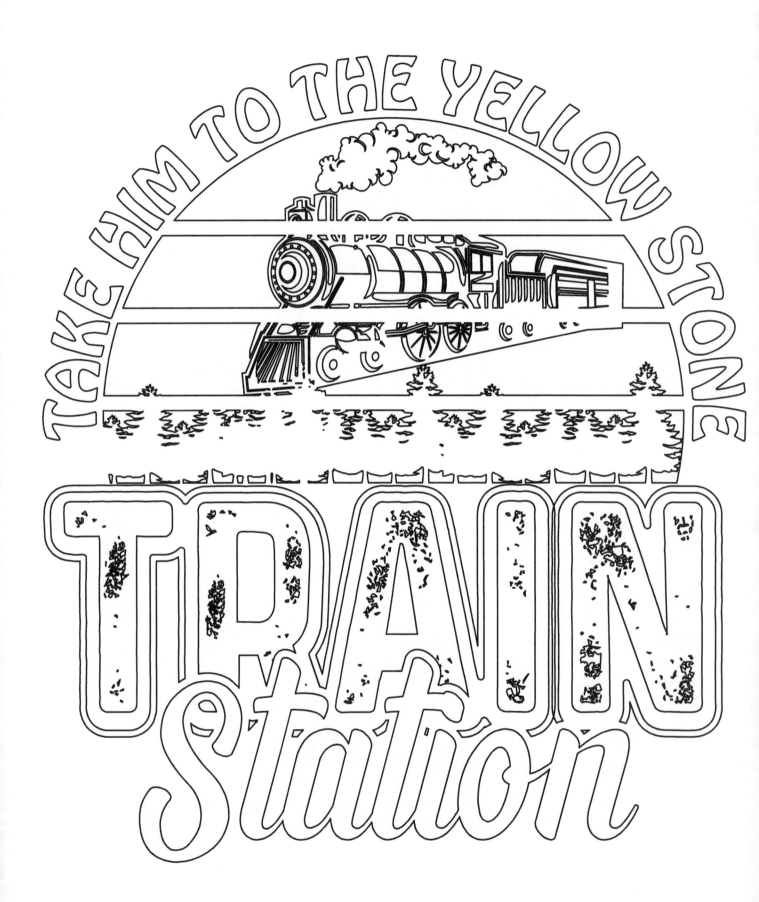

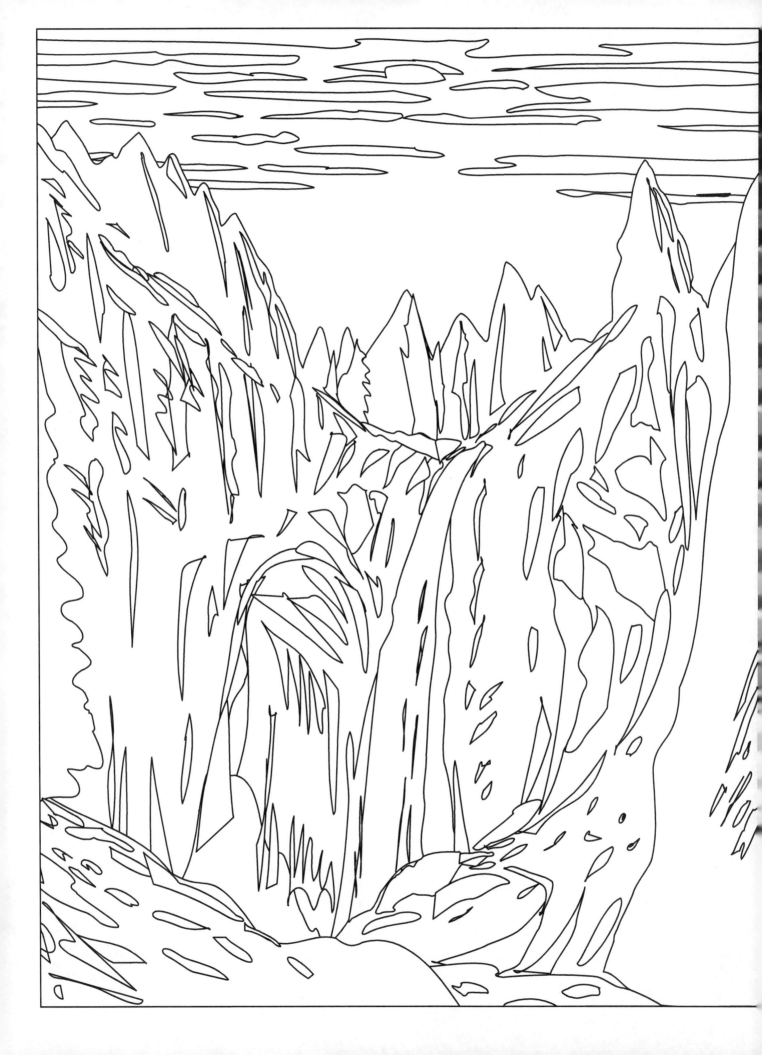

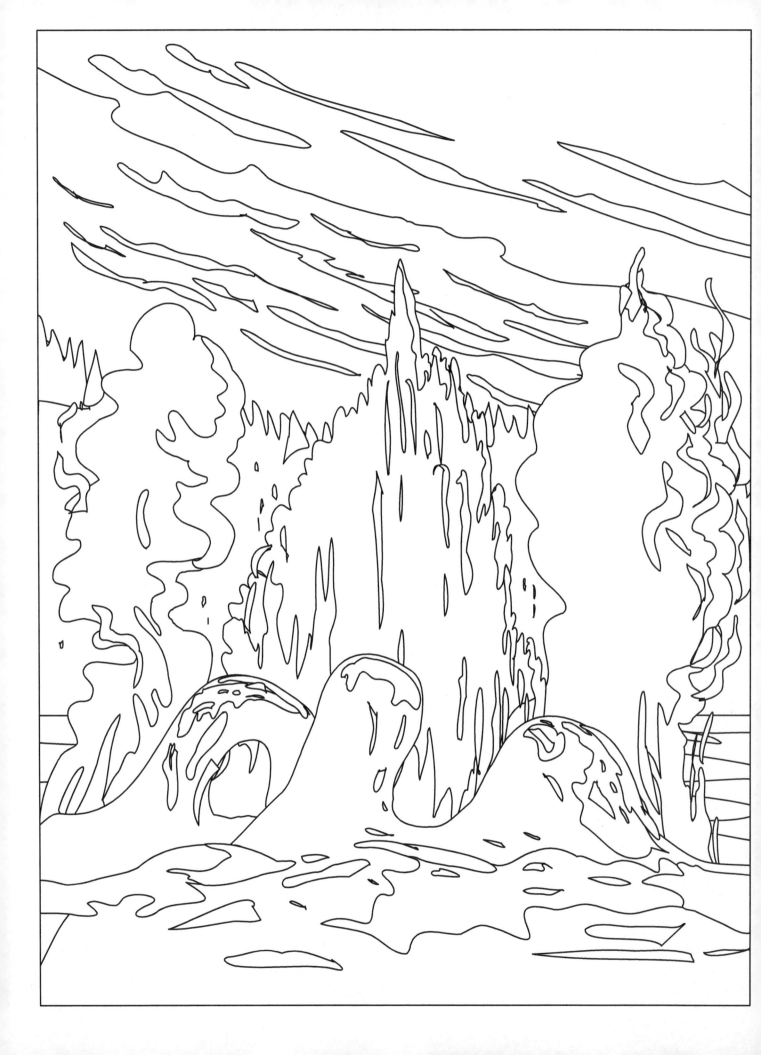

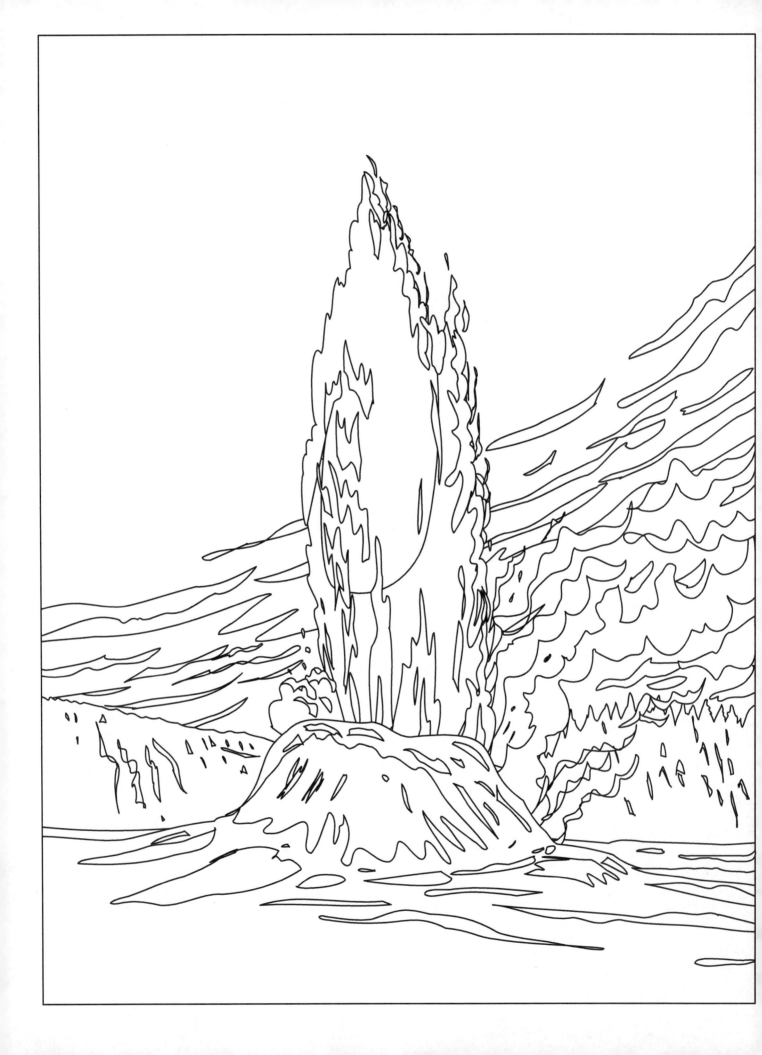

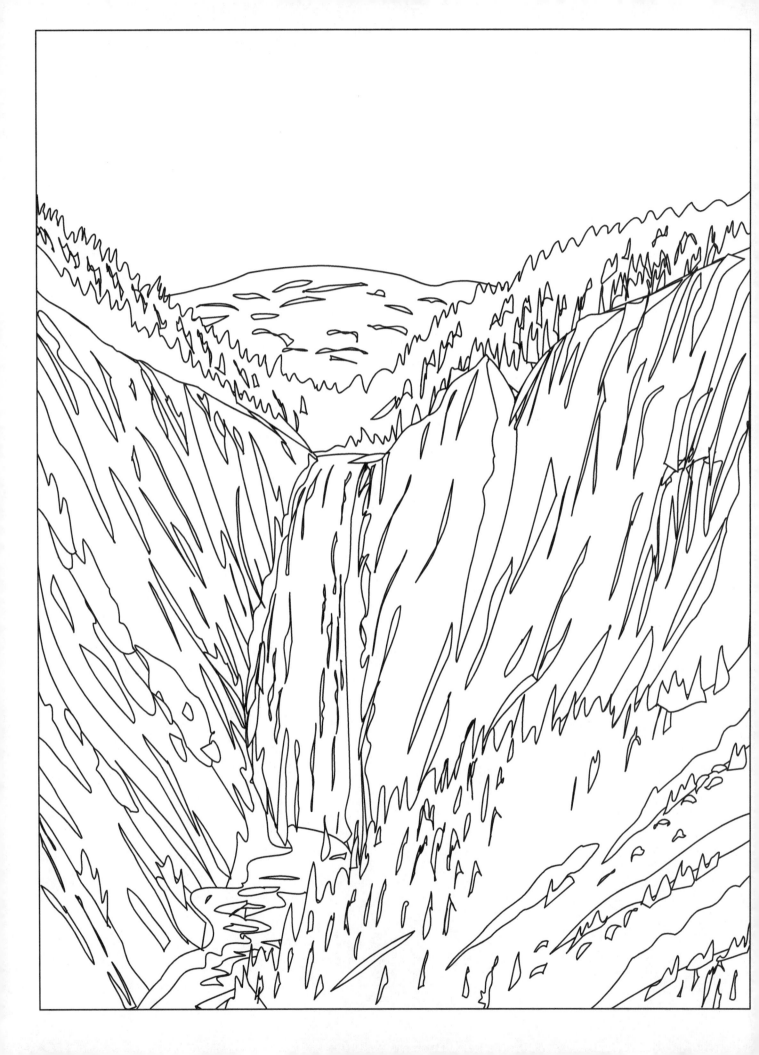

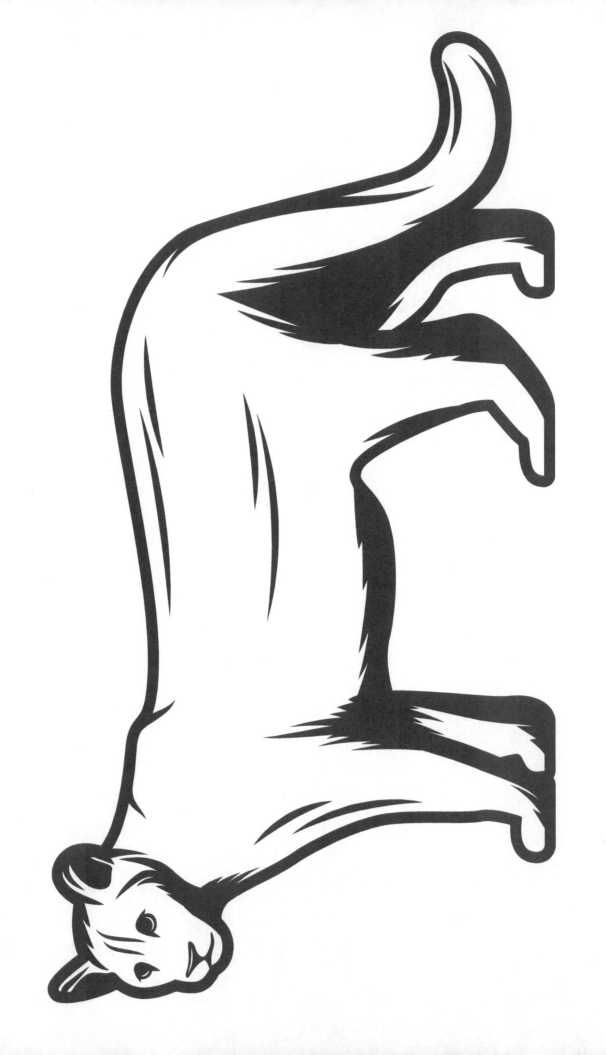

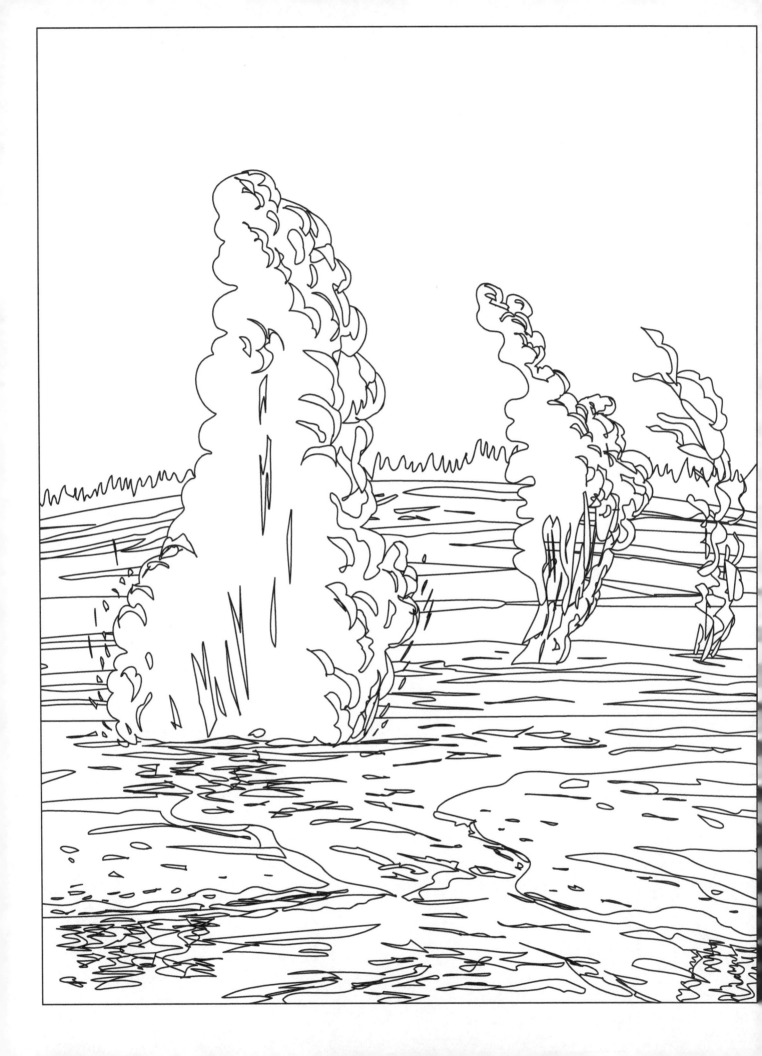

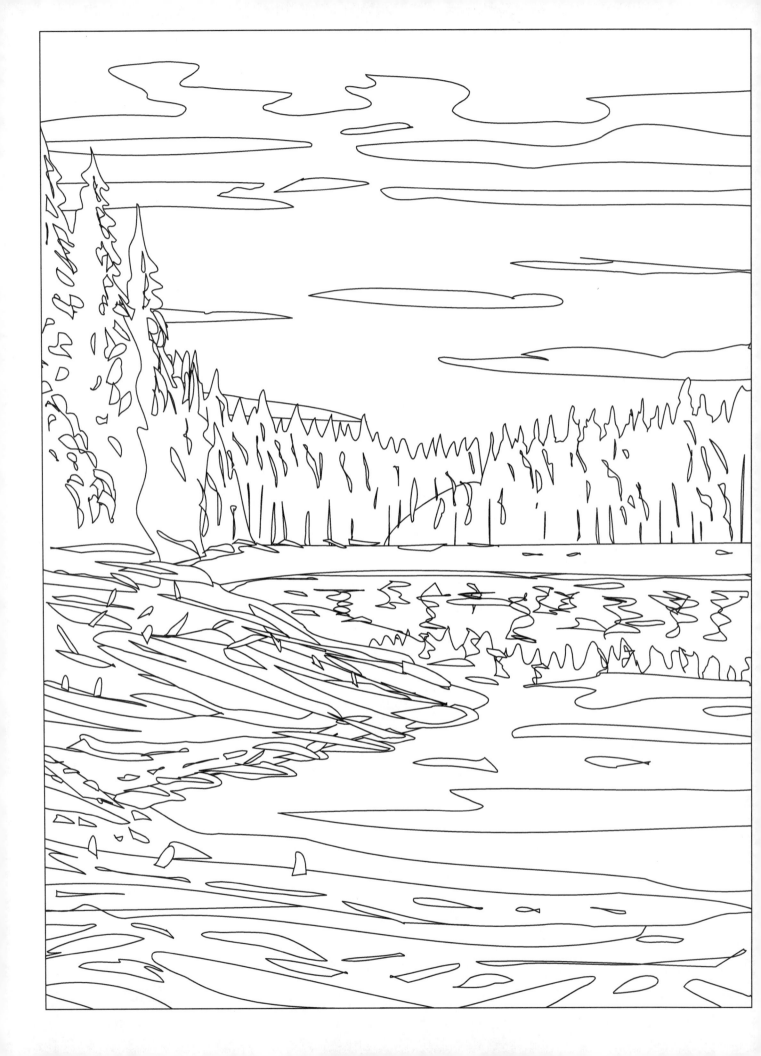

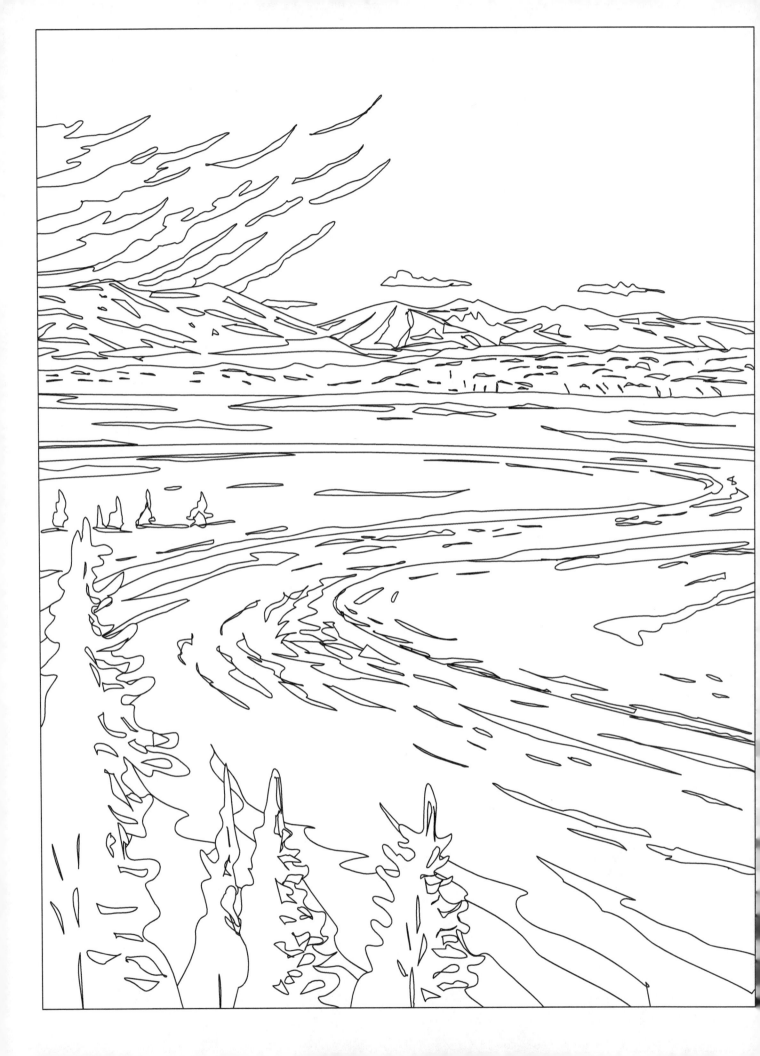

Made in United States
Troutdale, OR
03/11/2024